PIANO • VOCAL • GUITAR

DISNEY
SAVING MR. BANKS
MUSIC FROM THE MOTION PICTURE SOUNDTRACK

Disney characters and artwork © Disney Enterprises, Inc.

ISBN 978-1-4803-8309-8

Wonderland Music Company, Inc.

DISTRIBUTED BY

HAL • LEONARD®
CORPORATION

7777 W. BLUEMOUND RD. P.O. BOX 13819 MILWAUKEE, WI 53213

In Australia Contact:
Hal Leonard Australia Pty. Ltd.
4 Lentara Court
Cheltenham, Victoria, 3192 Australia
Email: ausadmin@halleonard.com.au

Visit Hal Leonard Online at
www.halleonard.com

CONTENTS

A SPOONFUL OF SUGAR

Words and Music by RICHARD M. SHERMAN
and ROBERT B. SHERMAN

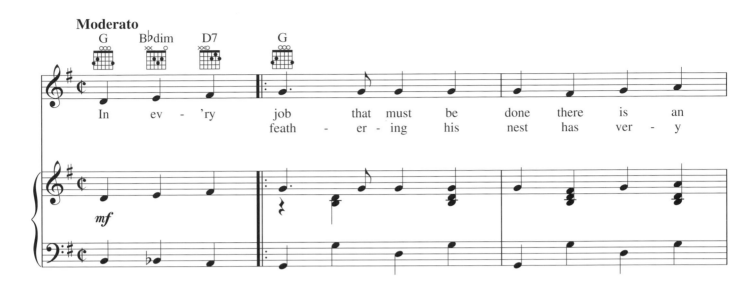

In ev - 'ry job that must be done there is an
feath - er - ing his done nest has ver - y

el - e - ment of fun; You find the fun and
lit - tle time to rest while find gath - er - ing his

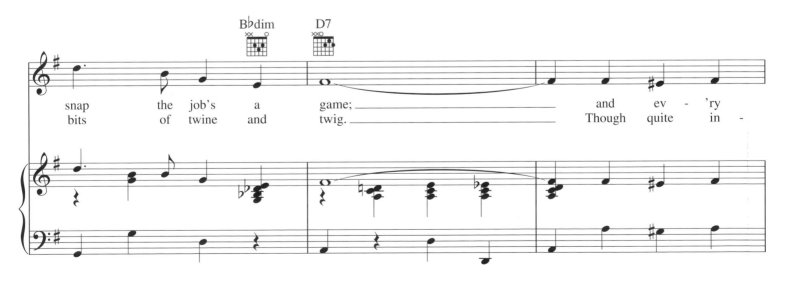

snap the job's a game; _____ and ev - 'ry
bits of twine and twig. _____ Though quite in -

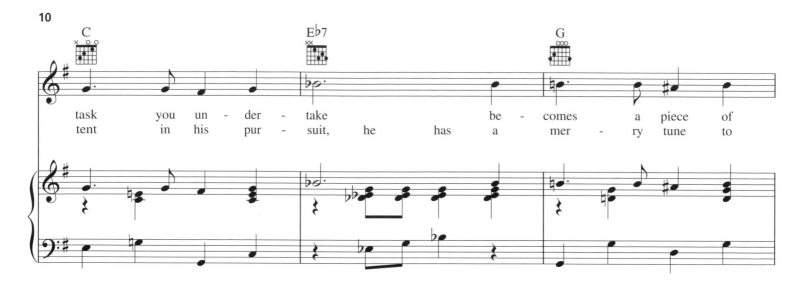

task you un - der - take be - comes a piece of
tent in his pur - suit, he has a mer - ry tune to

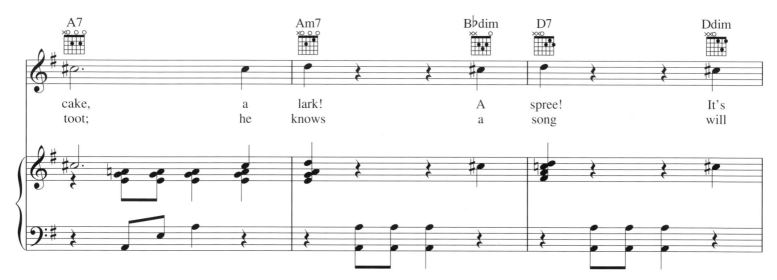

cake, a lark! A spree! It's
toot; he knows a song will

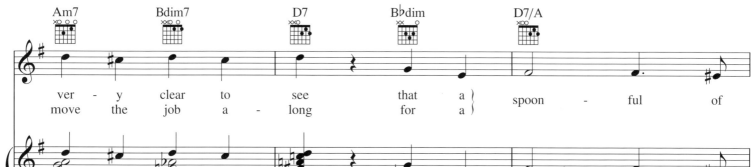

ver - y clear to see that a } spoon - ful of
move the job a - long for a }

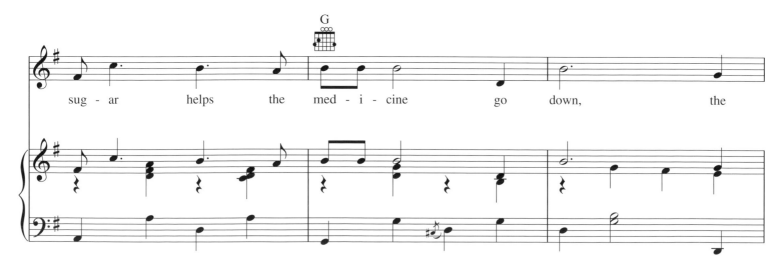

sug - ar helps the med - i - cine go down, the

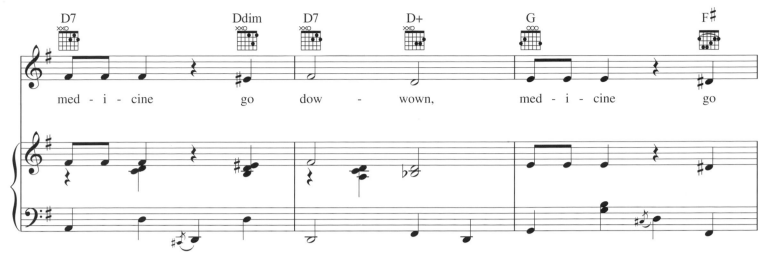

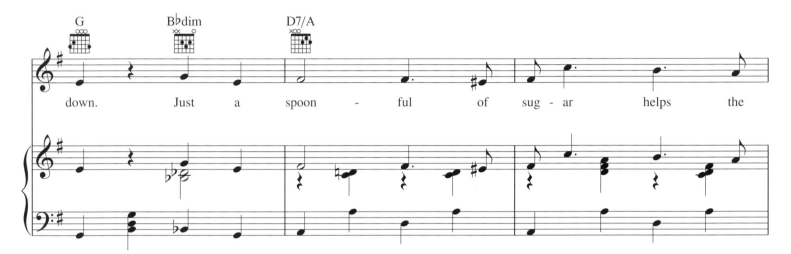

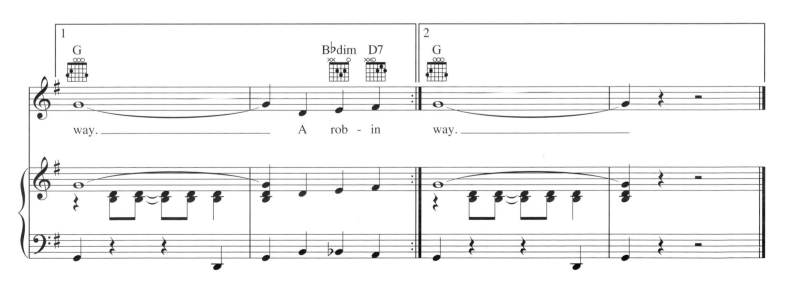

SUPERCALIFRAGILISTICEXPIALIDOCIOUS

Words and Music by RICHARD M. SHERMAN
and ROBERT B. SHERMAN

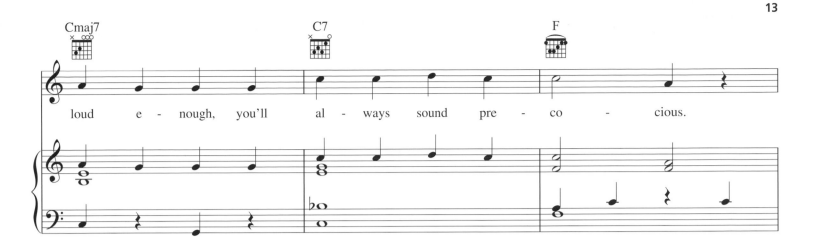

loud e - nough, you'll al - ways sound pre - co - cious.

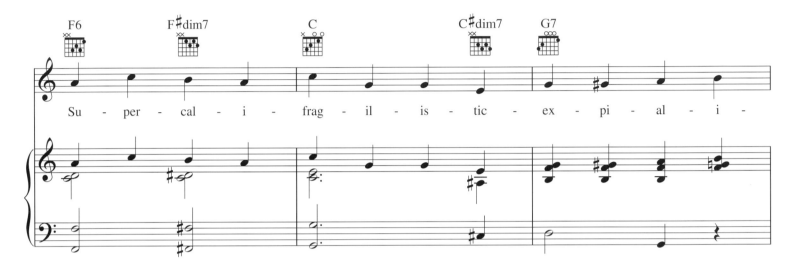

Su - per - cal - i - frag - il - is - tic - ex - pi - al - i -

do - cious! *Pearlies:* Um did - dle did - dle did - dle, um did - dle ay!

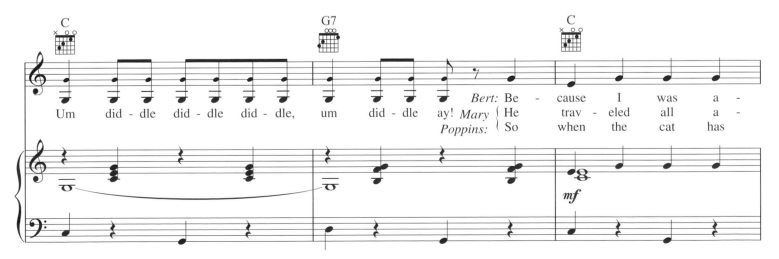

Um did - dle did - dle did - dle, um did - dle ay! *Bert:* Be - cause I was a -
Mary {He trav - eled all a -
Poppins: {So when the cat has

Cmaj7   C6   C#dim7   G7

fraid to speak When I was just a lad, Me
round the world And ev - 'ry - where he went He'd
got your tongue, There's no need to dis - may. Just

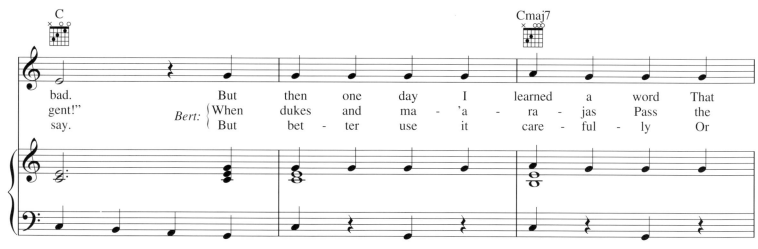

Dm7   G7   Dm7   G7

fa - ther gave me nose a tweak And told me I was
use his word and all would say, "There goes a clev - er
sum - mon up this word And then you've got a lot to

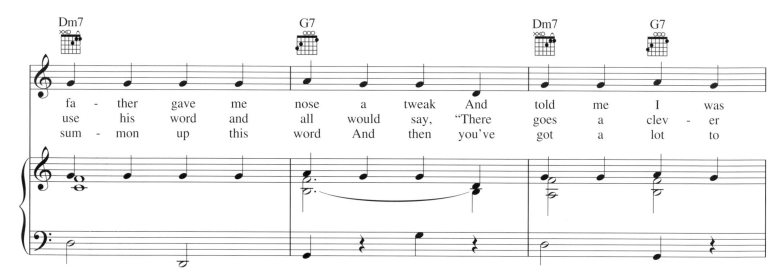

C   Cmaj7

bad.   *Bert:* { But then one day I learned a word That
gent!"   When dukes and ma - 'a - ra - jas Pass the
say.   But bet - ter use it care - ful - ly Or

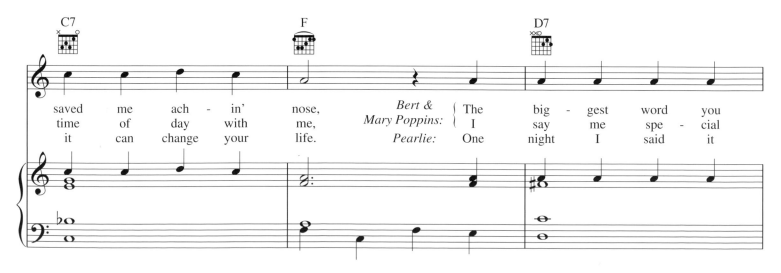

C7   F   D7

saved me ach - in' nose,   *Bert &* { The big - gest word you
time of day with me,   *Mary Poppins:* { I say me spe - cial
it can change your life.   *Pearlie:* One night I said it

ev - er 'eard And this is 'ow it goes: Oh!
word And then they ask me out to tea. *All:* Oh!
to me then girl And now me girl's me wife. *All:* She's

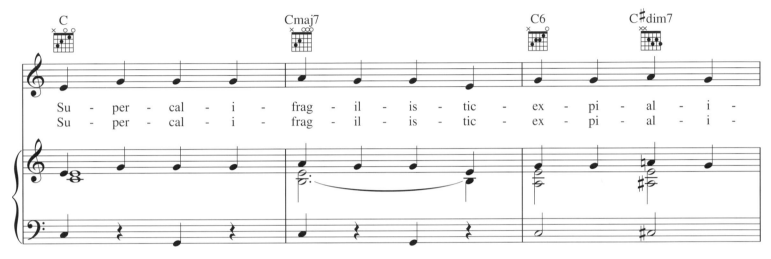

Su - per - cal - i - frag - il - is - tic - ex - pi - al - i -
Su - per - cal - i - frag - il - is - tic - ex - pi - al - i -

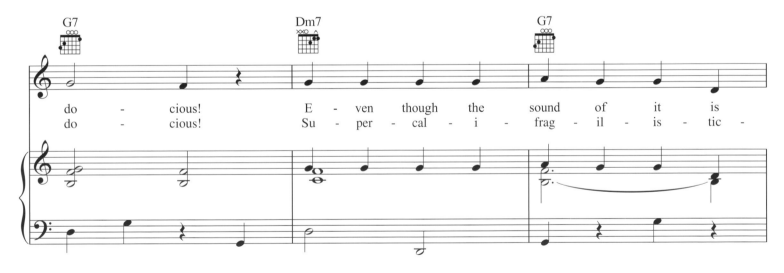

do - cious! E - ven though the sound of it is
do - cious! Su - per - cal - i - frag - il - is - tic -

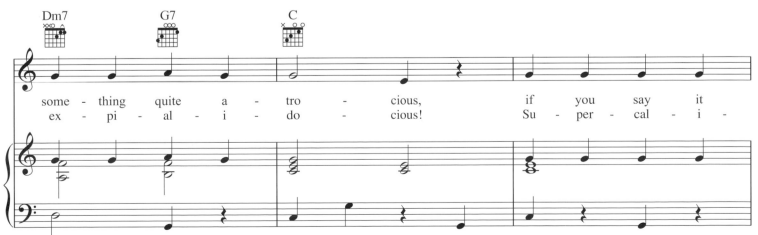

some - thing quite a - tro - cious, if you say it
ex - pi - al - i - do - cious! Su - per - cal - i -

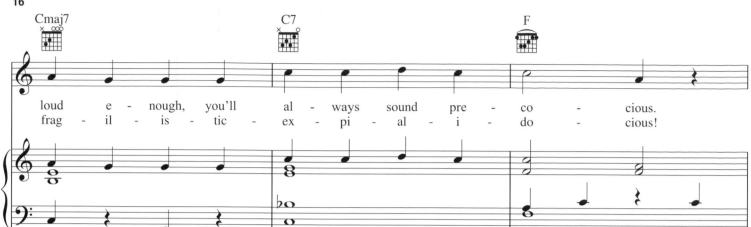

loud e - nough, you'll al - ways sound pre - co - cious.
frag - il - is - tic - ex - pi - al - i - do - cious!

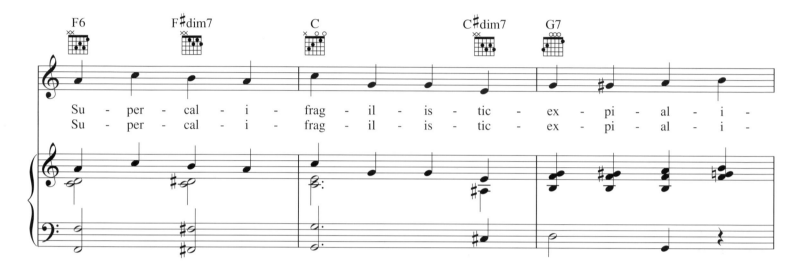

Su - per - cal - i - frag - il - is - tic - ex - pi - al - i -
Su - per - cal - i - frag - il - is - tic - ex - pi - al - i -

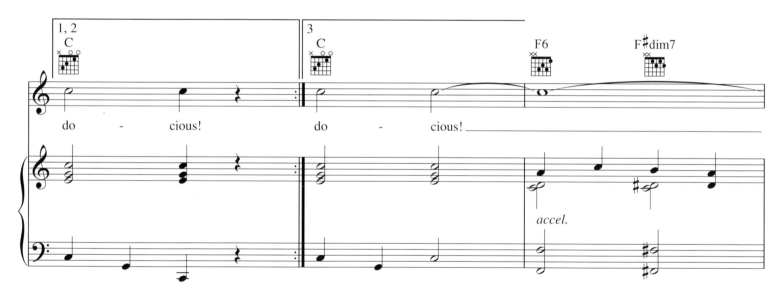

do - cious! do - cious! _____

accel.

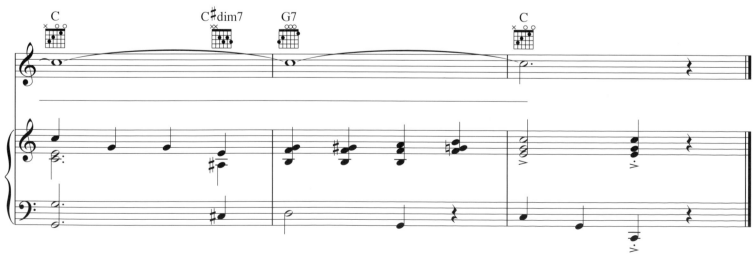

CHIM CHIM CHER-EE

Words and Music by RICHARD M. SHERMAN
and ROBERT B. SHERMAN

off   when I   shakes 'ands   with   you,   or   blow   me   a   kiss   and

that's   luck - y,   too.

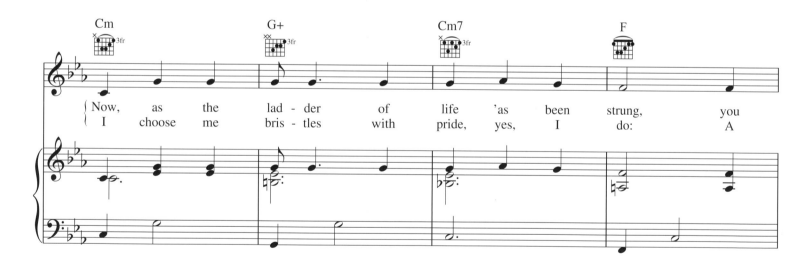

Now,   as   the   lad - der   of   life   'as   been   strung,   you
I   choose   me   bris - tles   with   pride,   yes,   I   do: A

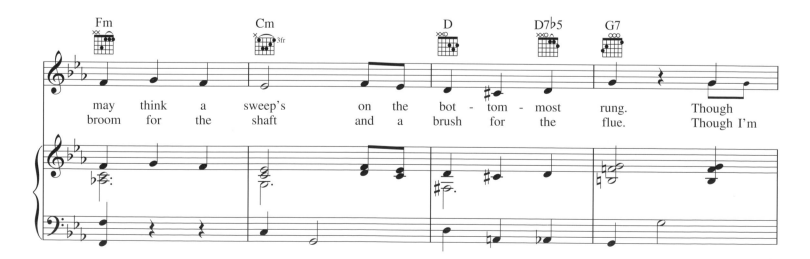

may   think   a   sweep's   on   the   bot - tom - most   rung.   Though
broom   for   the   shaft   and   a   brush   for   the   flue.   Though I'm

I spends me time in the ash - es and smoke, in
cov - ered with time soot from me 'ead to me toes, a

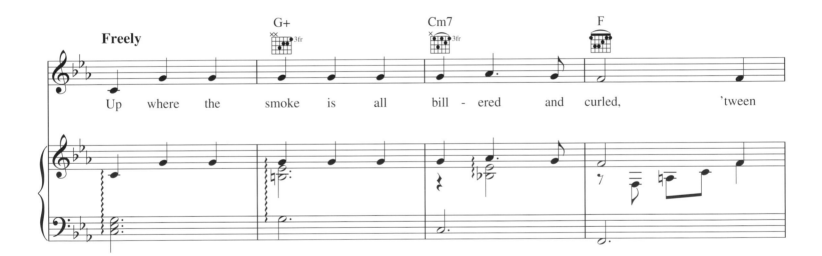

this 'ole wide world there's no 'ap - pi - er bloke.
sweep knows 'e's wel - come wher - ev - er 'e goes.

Freely

Up where the smoke is all bill - ered and curled, 'tween

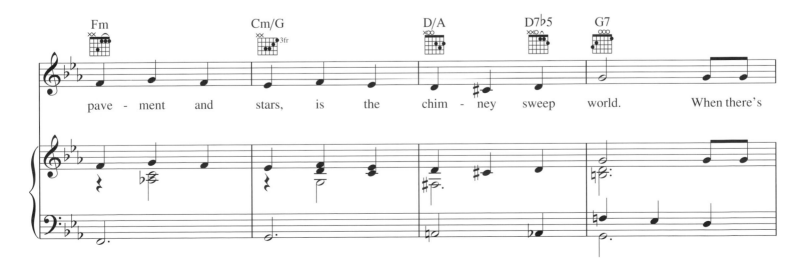

pave - ment and stars, is the chim - ney sweep world. When there's

'ard - ly no day nor 'ard - ly no night, there's

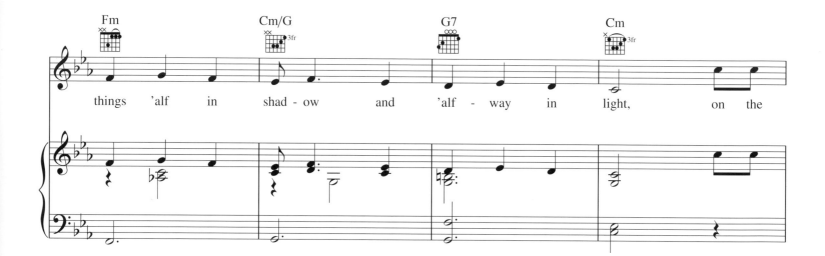

things 'alf in shad - ow and 'alf - way in light, on the

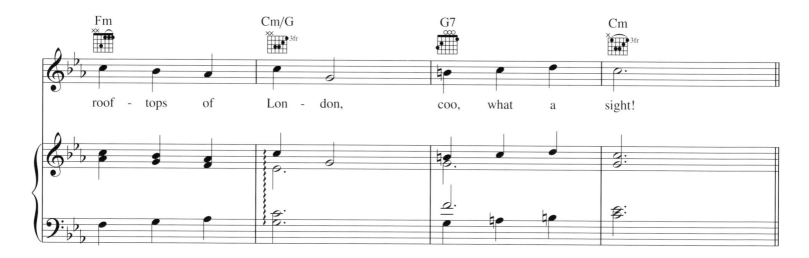

roof - tops of Lon - don, coo, what a sight!

Tempo I

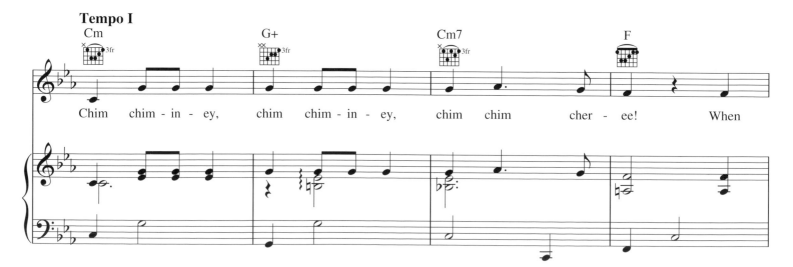

Chim chim - in - ey, chim chim - in - ey, chim chim cher - ee! When

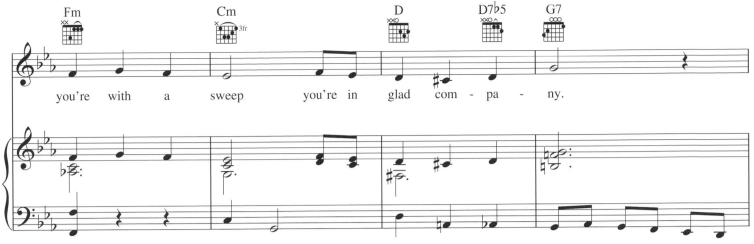

you're with a sweep you're in glad com-pa-ny.

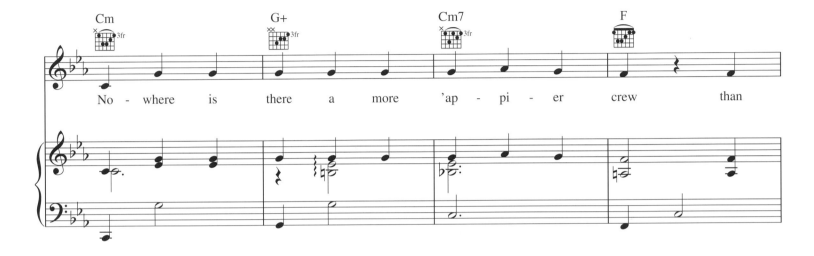

No - where is there a more 'ap - pi - er crew than

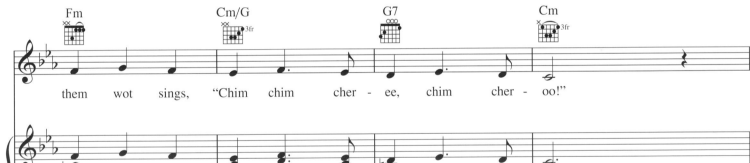

them wot sings, "Chim chim cher - ee, chim cher - oo!"

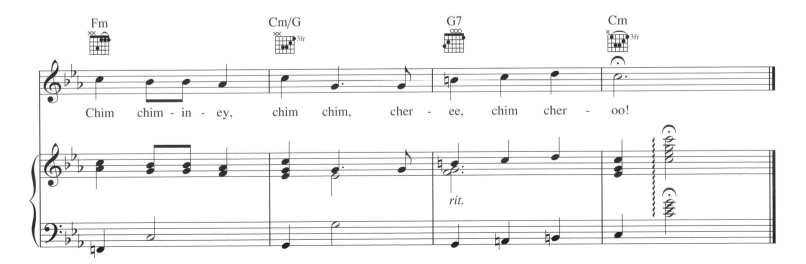

Chim chim-in-ey, chim chim, cher - ee, chim cher - oo!

rit.

FEED THE BIRDS

Words and Music by RICHARD M. SHERMAN
and ROBERT B. SHERMAN

Slowly, with feeling

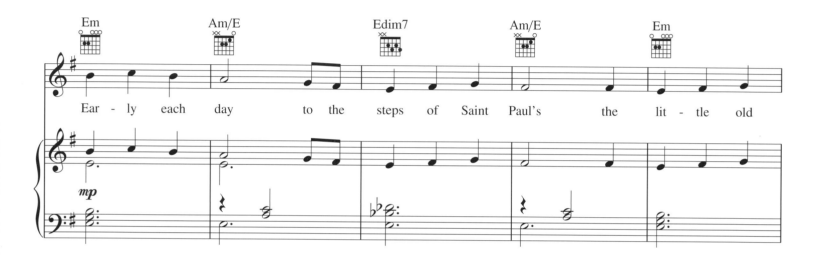

Ear- ly each day to the steps of Saint Paul's the lit- tle old

bird wom- an comes. _____ In her own spe- cial

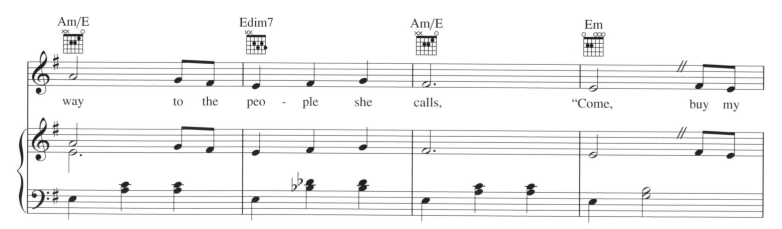

way to the peo- ple she calls, "Come, buy my

bags full of crumbs._____ Come feed the

lit - tle birds, show them you care, and you'll be

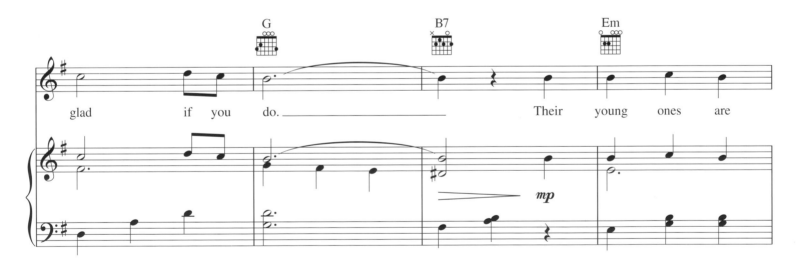

glad if you do._____ Their young ones are

hun - gry, their nests are so bare; all it takes is tup - pence from

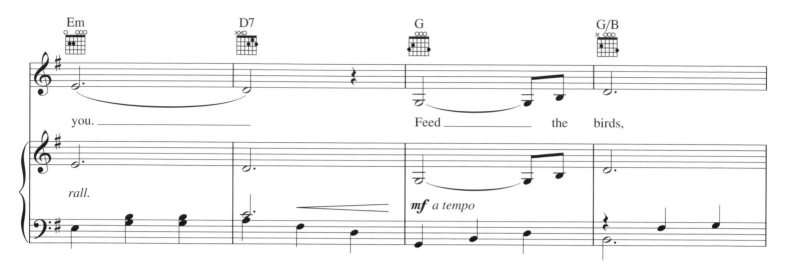

you. _____ Feed _____ the birds,

rall.   **mf** *a tempo*

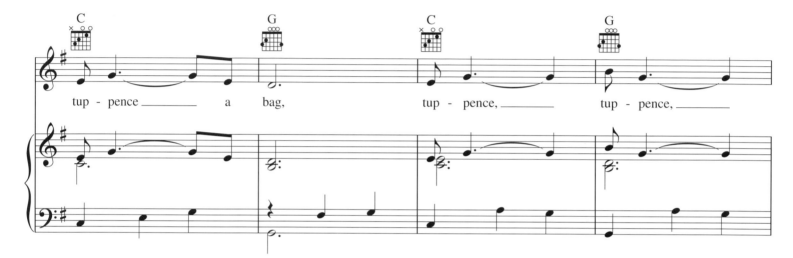

tup - pence _____ a bag,   tup - pence, _____   tup - pence, _____

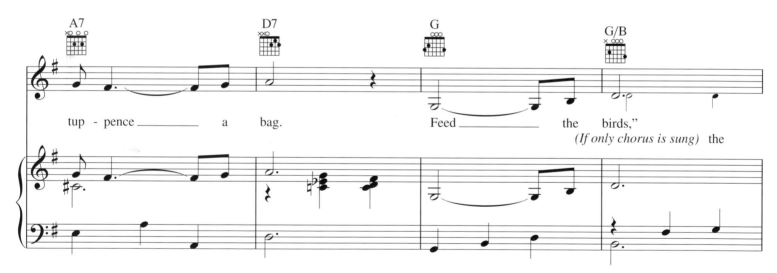

tup - pence _____ a bag.   Feed _____ the birds,"

(If only chorus is sung) the

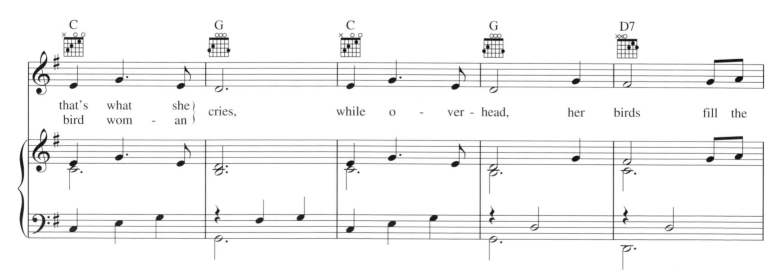

that's what she } cries,   while o - ver - head, her birds fill the
bird wom - an

Slightly faster

skies. All a - round the ca - the - dral the saints and a -

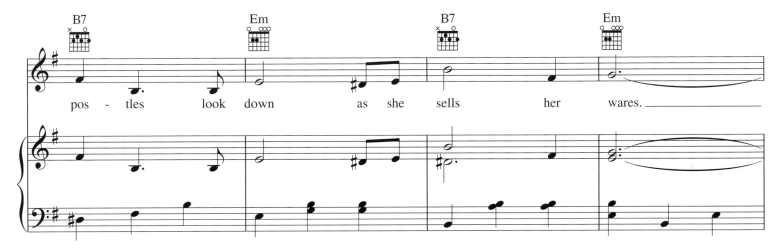

pos - tles look down as she sells her wares.

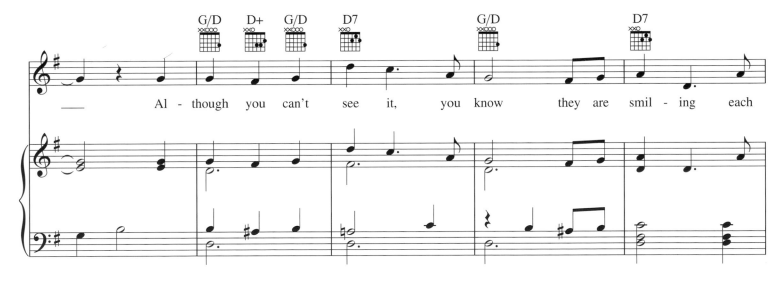

— Al - though you can't see it, you know they are smil - ing each

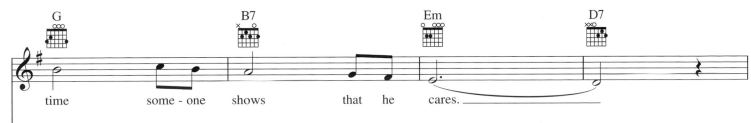

time some - one shows that he cares.

rit.

Tempo I

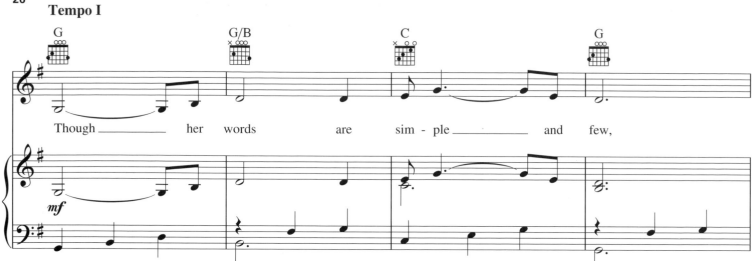

Though _____ her words are sim - ple _____ and few,

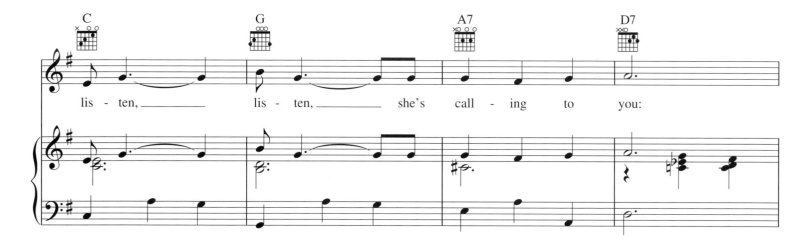

lis - ten, _____ lis - ten, _____ she's call - ing to you:

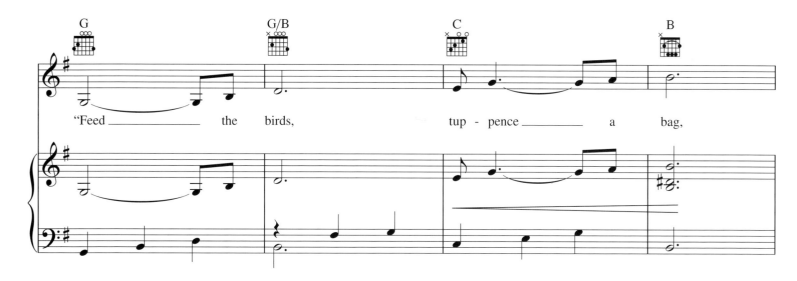

"Feed _____ the birds, tup - pence _____ a bag,

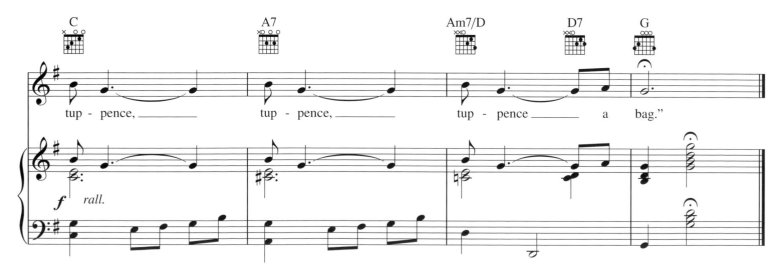

tup - pence, _____ tup - pence, _____ tup - pence _____ a bag."

LET'S GO FLY A KITE

Words and Music by RICHARD M. SHERMAN
and ROBERT B. SHERMAN

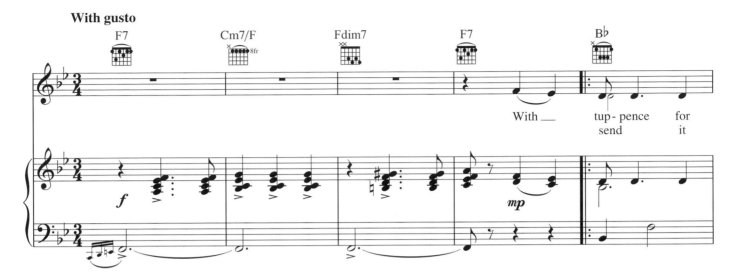

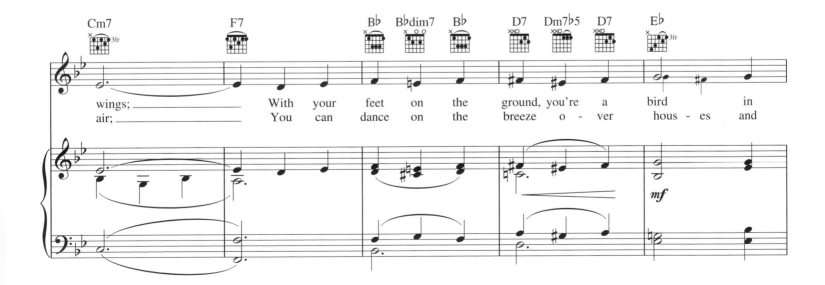

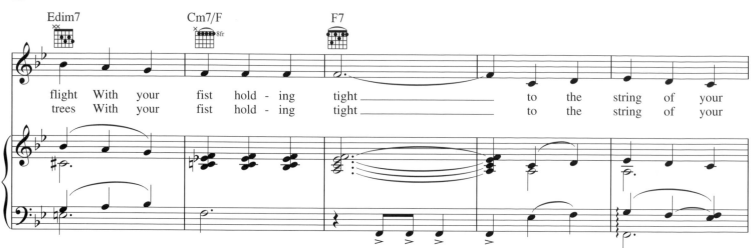

flight With your fist hold-ing tight _____ to the string of your
trees With your fist hold-ing tight _____ to the string of your

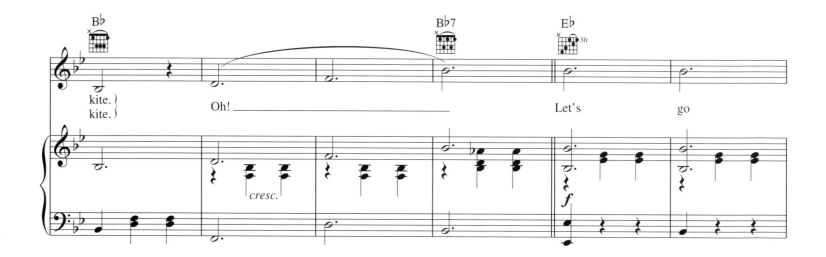

kite. }
kite. }
Oh! _____
Let's go

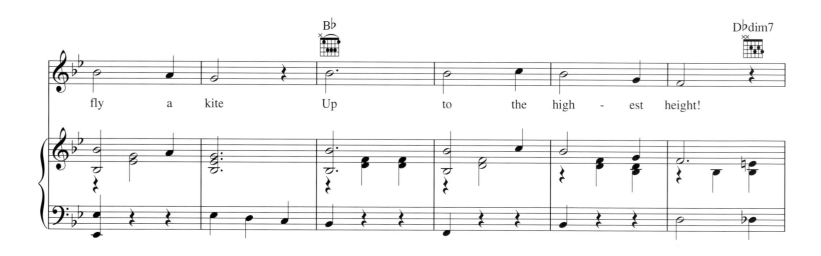

fly a kite Up to the high-est height!

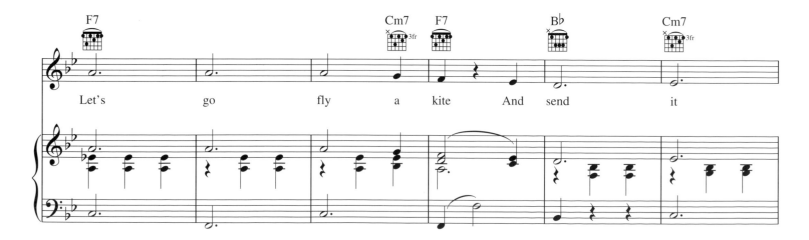

Let's go fly a kite And send it

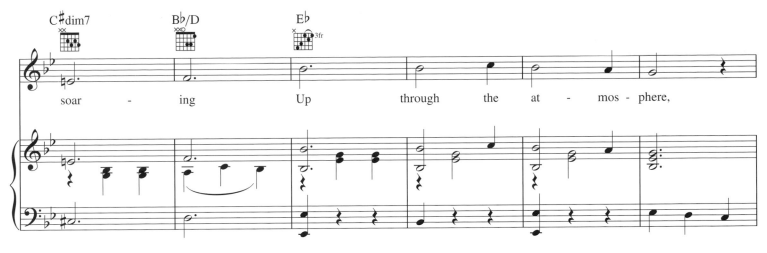

soar - ing Up through the at - mos - phere,

Up where the air is clear. Oh, let's

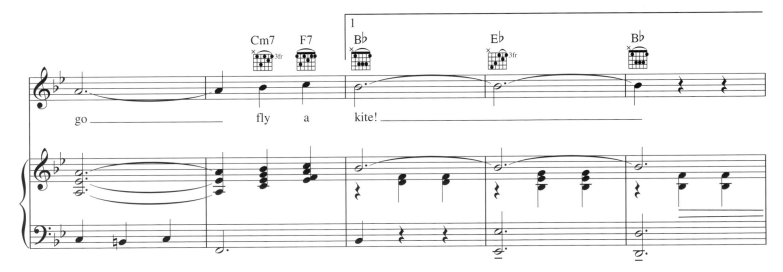

go _____ fly a kite! _____

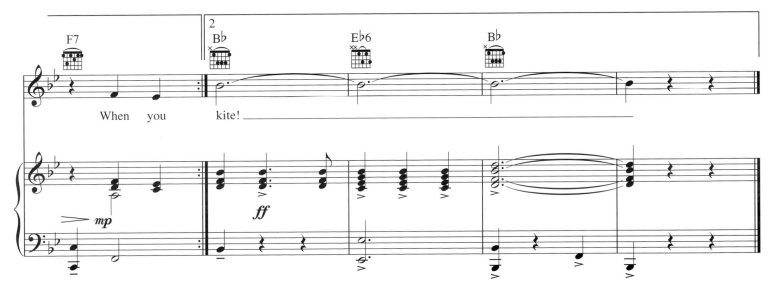

When you kite! _____

STEP IN TIME

Words and Music by RICHARD M. SHERMAN
and ROBERT B. SHERMAN

Spirited, with abandon

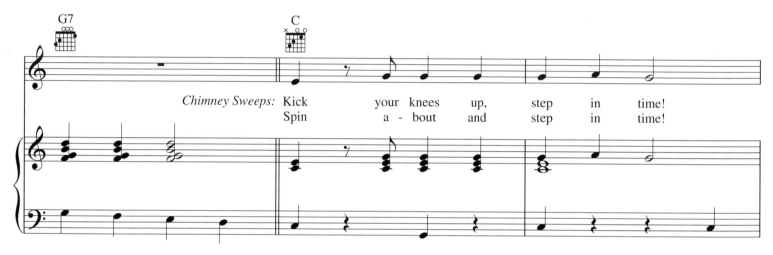

Chimney Sweeps: Kick your knees up, step in time!
Spin a - bout and step in time!

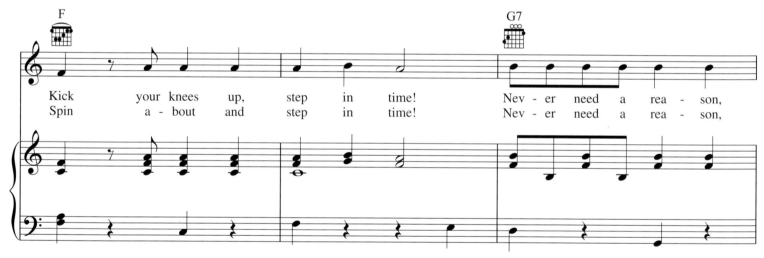

Kick your knees up, step in time! Nev - er need a rea - son,
Spin a - bout and step in time! Nev - er need a rea - son,

nev - er need a rhyme, kick your knees up, step in time!
nev - er need a rhyme, spin a - bout and step in time!

Link your el - bows, step in time! Link your el - bows,
'Round the chim - ney, step step in time! 'Round the chim - ney,

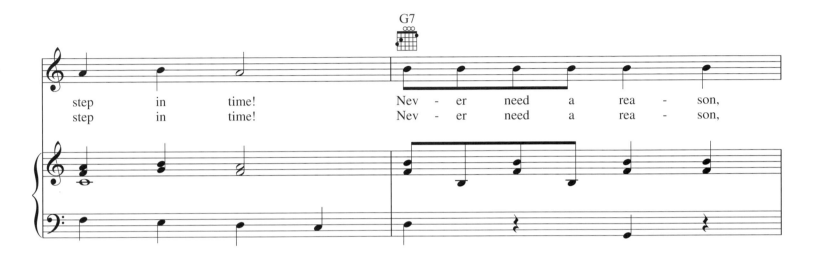

step in time! Nev - er need a rea - son,
step in time! Nev - er need a rea - son,

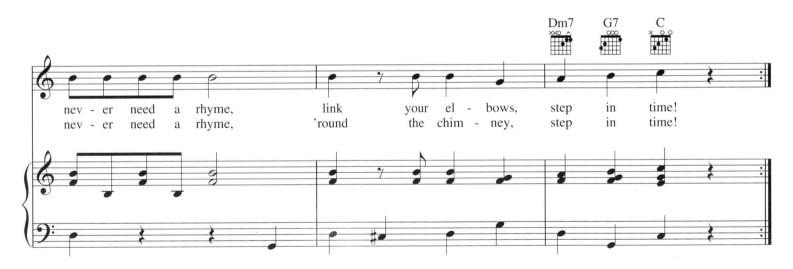

nev - er need a rhyme, link your el - bows, step in time!
nev - er need a rhyme, 'round the chim - ney, step in time!

N.C.

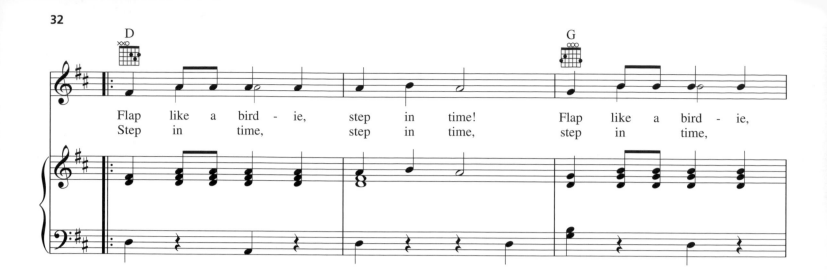

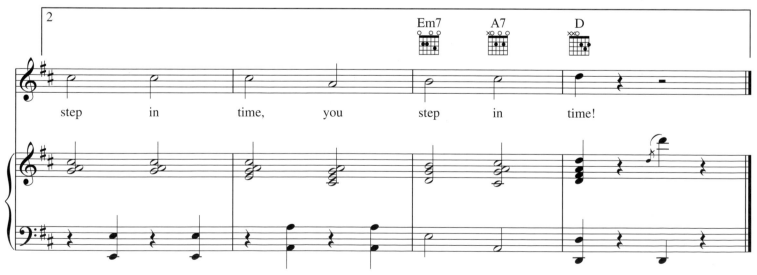